SPIRITUALLY
WOKE

SPIRITUALLY
WOKE

A Journey to
Spiritual Awareness and Inspiration

7 Principles
7 Weeks

DR. SUNNE-RYSE S. SMITH

Copyright © 2019 by Dr. Sunne-Ryse S. Smith.
All rights reserved. No part of this book may be reproduced in any written, electronic, recording, or photocopying without written permission of the publisher or author. The exception would be in the case of brief quotations embodied on the pages where the publisher or author specifically grants permission.
Books may be purchased in quantity and/or special sales by contacting the publisher.

Mynd Matters Publishing
715 Peachtree Street NE, Suites 100 & 200, Atlanta, GA 30308
www.myndmatterspublishing.com

ISBN-13: 978-1-948145-24-4 (pbk) | 978-1-948145-28-2 (eBook)

FIRST EDITION

To Kyle, my best friend with benefits, prayer partner, personal entertainment, and biggest cheerleader.

To say I could not do this without you would be an understatement. You have sacrificed and given of your time, career, financial security, and emotional strength. Thank you for saying "yes" to all of my ideas; God-led and some not so God-led!

To my two beautiful children: Sana'a and Lyfe.

In one week, at separate times, you each prophesied that I needed to leave my job. When I did not listen, God took control. Thank you for trusting your "gut" and speaking honestly to me. Thank you for choosing me to be your mom. I am a better woman because you teach me how to be a mother. God has His hand in your lives and I cannot wait to see His plans for you!

Kyle, Sana'a, and Lyfe,
Thank you for making me feel loved, powerful and happy!

"I've learned that people will forget what you said, people will forget what you did, but people will never forget how you made them feel."

—Dr. Maya Angelou

Contents

Foreword 11
Preface 13
Introduction 17
PRINCIPLE ONE: BELIEVE 27
PRINCIPLE TWO: SENSES 39
PRINCIPLE THREE: GRATITUDE 51
PRINCIPLE FOUR: THOUGHTS 63
PRINCIPLE FIVE: WORDS 77
PRINCIPLE SIX: TRANSFORMATION 91
PRINCIPLE SEVEN: CONTRIBUTION 105
SPIRITUALLY WOKE PRINCIPLES 119
FINAL THOUGHT 121
About the Author 123
What's Next? 125

Foreword

Sunrise: the time in early morning when the sun first appears in the sky with the light of a new day.

Instead of looking inward, we often seek fulfillment outside of ourselves. However, living in an awakened state on the inside is the key to experiencing a joyful, fulfilled, and enriching life. To be fully present and alert in every moment is a power we all possess but due to our busy lives, seldom use. The moment of awakening is like a sunrise when the light of a new morning pierces the clouds indicating it's a new day with new possibilities and new life. *Spiritually Woke* is that sunrise. It is a wake-up call drawing you closer and deeper to your authentic self and an inspired life.

What follows on subsequent pages is a guide to help on your journey of living a spiritually woke life. Dr. Sunne-Ryse will challenge you to think with a new mindset, guide you in ways that will shed light, and open you up to the Spirit and new levels of personal power.

In life, there are no coincidences. Dr. Sunne-Ryse lives up to her name by bringing illumination of a new day through the pages of this simple, yet deeply reflective, spiritual journey. I have had the privilege of mentoring her, through personal and professional development, over many years. She embodies the work of spiritual transformation. She is passionate about breathing new life into people and on several occasions, I have witnessed her speak to the spirit of people and shine a spotlight on their dreams and aspirations.

Through *Spiritually Woke*, you will gain access to the necessary tools to live spiritually aware. The straightforward information and practical strategies Dr. Sunne-Ryse shares are priceless. Give yourself the gift of living an awakened life, because never forget, you only have one.

Sylvia High
Aiming High, Inc.

Preface

"Any religion that professes to be concerned about the souls of men and is not concerned about the slums that damn them, the economic conditions that strangle them and the social conditions that cripple them is a spiritually moribund religion awaiting burial."

–Dr. Martin Luther King, Jr.

Spiritually Woke was born out of my desire for people to be spiritually aware and inspired to live each day with faith and social consciousness. I grew up in a home where our belief in God was manifested in our service to others. I watched my mom organize mentoring programs in Brooklyn, New York, for youth and create health walks to promote physical and spiritual wellness in urban communities. Although a Christian pastor now, I remember stories of when she and my dad were part of the Nation of Islam. My parents were always progressive in their thinking—my first examples of being *spiritually woke*. Before Dr. Martin Luther King, Jr's birthday became a federal holiday, they kept me and my brothers home from school. They believed Dr. King's work was God's work and it should be honored. My mom dared the school to mark us absent. She is still a firecracker to this day.

On the following pages, I vulnerably share what I have come to know as an ordained minister, Doctor of Psychology, daughter, wife, mother, and mentor, in hopes that you too will allow yourself to be vulnerable and make room for God to speak to you. I've included practices and teachings that contributed to my growth with the hope that they will spark something in you. Behind these words are my deepest desires for people to come from behind the veil of religion and connect with God in a tangible, intentional, and substantive way. The world needs more people who "walk by faith" from a place of love and responsibility–breathing life into other people's lives. I aim to come to you, not from a place of judgment and arrogance, but from a deep place of love and compassion.

My mom always says, "When you know better, you do better." I have learned so much about myself over the last forty-two years. As God grants me wisdom, I strive to *do* better.

"The biggest problem facing the world today is not people dying in the streets of Calcutta, and not inflation, but spiritual deprivation...this feeling of emptiness associated with feeling separate from God, and from all other sisters and brothers on planet Earth."

—Mother Teresa

Introduction

"In the midst of outer dangers, I have felt an inner calm and known resources of strength that only God could give. In many instances, I have felt the power of God transforming the fatigue of despair into the buoyancy of hope. I am convinced that the universe is under the control of a loving purpose and that in the struggle for righteousness man has cosmic companionship.

–Dr. Martin Luther King Jr.

Have you ever laid in bed at night and wondered whether God could hear you? Have you ever felt a nudging in your gut that the path you were on was not right for you? Has there ever been a day where you felt empty inside, but did not know where to find inspiration or purpose? Some of these moments may have been triggered by personal loss, financial distress, professional uncertainty, or health challenges. But the truth is, you are not alone. From the time you are born until you transcend your physical body, you will struggle with life experiences that will require you to do an internal audit of your thoughts and behaviors. These internal audits are an integral part of your spiritual development because you learn about the transforming power of God and His power to transform your life from despair to hope.

The great revelation of it all is that feeling uninspired or thinking you are on the wrong path has more to do with what is happening inside of you than what is happening around you. Consider that God is always communicating with you. The circumstances you face are indicators, no different from the notifications you receive on the navigation system in your car. You were created to live an inspired life and when that is not occurring you feel out of alignment. The life you are drawn to and the life you are living should be one in the same. When you are misaligned, you will have breath but not be alive.

**Woke = Aware of and actively attentive to important facts and issues around you
(especially issues of racial and social justice)**

Genesis 2:7 states, "God formed man from the dust of the ground and breathed into his nostrils the breath of life; and man became a living soul." From the time you took your first breath, your purpose was to be a "living soul" and not merely a breathing body. To be a living soul means to be awake or alert to life, an active participant in the life experience. Are you awake to your life? Are you living a life that inspires others? Have you been attentive to why and for *whom* God gave you breath?

As a baby, when you were hungry you were aware of your environment such as how you felt and how people around you responded to your behaviors, like crying. You quickly learned how to get your need for food met. As you matured, your hunger took on different forms. You went from only needing to be physically fed to needing to be spiritually fed and nurtured.

Being "woke" is a spiritual experience. Living your life with purpose and inspiration will require your sight to mature beyond the physical world. You were created to be an answer to someone's prayer.

> **"Your life is the answer to someone's unanswered prayer."**
> –Dr. Sunne-Ryse Smith

As far back as I can remember, I have always been sensitive to people's emotions, words, and behaviors. It was something I felt but could never understand. Crying at commercials or TV shows often made me the brunt of jokes. As I matured spiritually, I learned my unique gift had nothing to do with me. I realized my name *and* the circumstances of my birth were indicators of God's divine plan to use my life for His purpose and I believe God is calling for you to be aware of your talents and personal story so you can be a blessing to someone as well.

My mother named me Sunne-Ryse (*pronounced: Sunrise*) because God instructed her to do so. One morning, during a period of despair and in the midst of her pregnancy with me, she prayed a simple prayer while sitting in Prospect Park. "God, should I have this child?" She asked with a spirit of expectancy because she trusted God to answer. As the sun began to rise, God told her, "Name her Sunrise for she will be the dawning of a new day to everyone she meets and bring joy to your life." I realized early on that my life was not just about me but about the people who God wants me to inspire. If you are reading this book, that is you!

> **"You're waiting on God to show up.**
> **He is waiting for you to grow up."**
> 			–Pastor Steven Furtick

Spiritually Woke is about more than religious belief. Many people practice or are part of a religion but are not spiritually awake, which requires a certain level of maturity. It is about being cognizant of the breath God gives you every day and how that same breath can transform someone else's life. It is about listening to your inner voice, your spirit, when it directs you to call someone who has been on your mind or to take a leap of faith to change careers. Being *spiritually woke* is about tending to your spirit so you can live a full, inspired life that benefits you *and* humankind. It is about your ability to listen to that still, small voice as it calls you to higher consciousness, rooted in God, and gives you the confidence to powerfully *choose* your life.

> **"Don't be like a walking dead person – wake up from the coma you're in and start living and impacting the world around you."**
>
> –Dr. Cindy Trimm

In this age of trendy weight loss programs, where a tea, body shaper, or fad diet is pitched as the way to get your body "snatched," one can forget about the non-physical parts of us like our spirit. There is such an emphasis on external appearance including, the size and shape of your body, the designer labels you wear, the type of car you drive or how many likes you have on a social media post.

Prioritizing these things will cause us to neglect the essence of who we are as human beings. We can forget that our bodies are meant to be carriers of our purpose, gifts, dreams, and passions. Without inspiration (to blow into, breathe upon) and divine influence from God, the body would have nothing to do but walk aimlessly through the world.

Moments of uncertainty, disappointment, and discouragement can be your greatest moments of spiritual awakening. Through them, you can experience God in new ways and evolve as a person. You may currently be in a period of growth or maybe you are in search of inspiration. Perhaps you are transitioning in your personal life and you're being drawn to a new career path or you have experienced a loss and are navigating a new normal. These "wake-up calls" are God's way of helping you recalibrate, reset, and resuscitate your spirit.

> **"Time and again, I have heard deep callings that felt inevitable and which I could have ignored, but only at great risk of something essential perishing."**
>
> **–Mark Nepo**

My wake-up call came when I was terminated from my job. While I was walking around among the land of the living, I behaved as though I was dead. Day in and day out I would go through my routine, shutting out any and everything that appeared to be a distraction. I was silencing my spirit while also ignoring signs that my spirit was being neglected and had become, what I call, "spiritually anemic." Spiritual anemia is when the spirit isn't connected to God and does not receive oxygen (messages of hope, joy, gratitude, and love) which results in the body experiencing symptoms like fatigue, weakness, insomnia, and difficulty concentrating.

I became spiritually anemic. I stopped dreaming and therefore, stopped living. My spiritual practices were erratic at best. I was alive, of course, because I was still breathing. But I was dead on the inside. My physical body began to break down through back pain, weight gain, irregular sleep patterns, and low energy.

Then, in an instant, that experience you know is possible but never really think about happening to you, happened. After giving all of my spiritual and emotional resources to my job, I was let go by my employer. Ironically, I was disappointed and relieved at the same time. While I felt as though a huge weight had been lifted and the excuses were taken away, I also felt disregarded because my efforts were not valued. The reality was I could no longer blame the position for my inability to write, create, and pursue the other plans God had for my life.

> "Your spirit is the part of you that is seeking meaning and purpose. That's one way someone can relate to that. Another way to understand spirit is that it's the part of you that is drawn to hope, that will not give in to despair. The part of you that has to believe in goodness—that has to believe in something more."
>
> –Caroline Myss

After losing my job, I began repairing the damage that had been done to my spirit. As God breathed His breath back into my body, I authored this book. It had been saved on my computer for almost a year. Scraps of paper here and there outlined my thoughts and revelations from God on how to inspire people to "wake up" to life. I allowed the uncertainty of unemployment and feeling unappreciated to become my inspiration. I was not ready to write *Spiritually Woke* before now because I was not awake to my own life.

I asked God to bless every page and for it to be the dawning of a new day for anyone who reads it. I prayed that people who were seeking inspiration and purpose would find their breath of life throughout the words.

As you take this journey, expect to be challenged through introspection and self-reflection. You must ask yourself some critical questions. Questions intended to awaken your spirit and support you in moving towards the life you desire. As you read each question, pause and think. Allow yourself a moment to be reflective and honest.

Before you begin, understand that to be fully awake to life requires your vulnerability and honestly. Proceed with an open heart and mind and allow yourself permission to peel away layers of thinking that may be hindering your spiritual growth. You will be amazed by the freedom available to you through a deeper connection with God.

It is a new day dawning! Are you ready? There is a new sunrise on the horizon. *Wake up!*

Tips to Get the Most Out of *Spiritually Woke*

1. Take a break from social media or limit the amount of time you spend "scrolling" through posts and profiles to a limited time period per day. Sometimes we need to reset our perspectives about life, so be intentional about how you spend your time. You will be surprised by what you learn about yourself.

2. Journaling can be very therapeutic so keep a journal and log your answers to each question and write down all thoughts and emotions that surface.

3. Take your time and be patient with yourself. *Spiritually Woke* is meant to stimulate your thinking and awaken you to new parts of yourself.

4. Go through this process with a friend or two as it helps to talk through the concepts and share your thoughts with others.

5. At the end of each section there are seven days of reflection and action, a "spiritual workout." Complete all the days because it is crucial to developing spiritual awareness. If you miss a day, pick up where you left off and begin again.

PRINCIPLE ONE: BELIEVE

"Trust in the Lord with all your heart and lean not on your own understanding. In all your ways acknowledge Him, and He will direct your path."

—Proverbs 3:5-6

Throughout the course of your life you will be faced with decisions that challenge you. You will be confronted with crossroads that do not have a clear path or obvious answer. You may even feel driven to take professional or financial risks to achieve an unbelievable goal. Have you ever felt compelled to do something that, to your friends and family, seemed far-fetched or impossible? When was the last time you had a dream or vision for yourself that was so great you were sure you could not accomplish it without divine intervention? Have you ever had a vision that terrified you? No great accomplishment comes without challenges that test you, your commitment, and your beliefs. It takes courage to follow a path that defies your own understanding.

The first principle is the foundation for all of the other principles in *Spiritually Woke*. Embrace the idea that there is a power in the universe that far exceeds our scientific theories. This power is experienced in those situations when you say, "Something in my gut didn't feel right," or "It was my intuition," or "My spirit was not comfortable." It is an intangible-tangible presence of a higher and greater power that pushes and pulls you emotionally, mentally, socially, and spiritually—the power of God. It is not always easy to explain because there is a fear of sounding "spooky" or crazy. Belief in God, however, has transformed people, families, communities, cities, countries, and the world, throughout history.

"...when you love and when you stand up to injustice, you are in that moment, bringing heaven to earth."
–Rob Bell

I often think about great men and women like Harriet Tubman, Dr. Martin Luther King Jr., Malcolm X, Rosa Parks, and Sojourner Truth. They were the epitome of *spiritually woke*. I reflect on the many paths and decisions each of them confronted, decisions we now know changed the course of history. Their willingness to stand up to injustice was the manifestation of God on Earth. What they were able to achieve in the times they lived could have only been divinely guided.

Who or what did they look to for guidance? How did they maintain their peace in the midst of chaos all around them? What gave them the courage and confidence to believe that they could achieve a vision and a dream that most of their peers thought was impossible? Imagine that! They faced countless crossroads and many individual decisions that ultimately affected the lives of people around the world. Could they have made such choices without holding a belief in something greater than themselves? Belief in God will inspire people to do great things, not in their own strength but through His.

> **"Use me, God. Show me how to take who I am, who I want to be, and what I can do, and use it for a purpose greater than myself."**
>
> **–Dr. Martin Luther King Jr.**

When I started working on my doctoral degree, I felt God directing me to complete it without taking on any school loans (yep, insert crazy face emoji.) Imagine it. I was still a young school psychologist fresh out of graduate school. I was about to marry my college sweetheart with whom I'd just purchased our first home and I did not have a permanent position at work.

Although the circumstances did not seem conducive to embark on a new academic or professional journey with new financial responsibilities, I could not shake the feeling that God was guiding me down that path. My question was, "Why couldn't it come with more money?" There were many days that it did not look like tuition would be paid or that the dissertation would be written but my belief in God inspired me to persevere.

I knew my degree would be used to accomplish good and there was a plan for my life far greater than what I thought. Through setbacks and tears, I continued to go back to that initial feeling that God was compelling me to follow this pathway. In May 2009, my belief in God took me across the stage at the Izod Center in New Jersey with my doctorate degree in psychology completed (with no school loans) and to the management of the social and emotional well-being of 40,000+ students in a large urban school district. God knew my beginning from my end. Even though I did not know where the journey would take me, I knew God had a plan.

"There is nothing on this Earth that compares with the power of belief. It is the belief that changes circumstances, alters destinies, and fuels miracles."

–Dr. Cindy Trimm

What do you believe the plan is for your life? Do you believe God is calling you to do something so great that it can only be accomplished through faith and trust in a higher power? Is there something tugging at your heart calling you to walk by faith for a greater good? The start of your journey begins here. As you watch the world around you, God is calling for people who are willing to follow that still, small voice. To be *spiritually woke* is to be aware of and believe in something higher and greater than yourself. To know that you possess a seed of purpose that, once planted, can and will transform the world!

Day 1: Believe

Spiritual Workout

1. What is the biggest vision you have for yourself and the people around you?
   - What would be one thing you would do if you knew you could not fail?
   - Why would you do that thing?
   - Why haven't you done it?
2. List some world-changing leaders you admire who have brought about positive transformation.
   - List the characteristics that helped them accomplish the unthinkable.
   - Did they believe in a higher power (i.e., God)?

Prayer

Dear God, help me trust you with all my heart. Increase my understanding of you and the plans you have for my life. Strengthen my ability to follow the path you set before me, even when it does not look clear. I believe you created me to do good on Earth. Today, I embrace your quiet directions and subtle signs to pursue that which I do not fully comprehend. Amen.

Day 2: Believe

Spiritual Workout

1. When was the last time you felt the pull to do something great but were too scared to pursue it?
   - What stopped you?
   - What do you need to take a leap of faith and follow that "pull"?
2. Write down all the risks you have wanted to take in the last year as it pertains to your career, personal life, and finances.
   - What was the motivation behind those risks?
   - For the risks you did not take, what has stopped you?

Prayer

Dear God, help me trust you with all my heart. Increase my understanding of you and the plans you have for my life. Strengthen my ability to follow the path you set before me, even when it does not look clear. I believe you created me to do good on Earth. Today I embrace your quiet directions and subtle signs to pursue that which I do not fully comprehend. Amen.

Day 3: Believe

Spiritual Workout

1. Why do you believe you were born?

   - What about your life experiences causes you to believe that about yourself?
   - Are you currently living a life that feels purposeful?

2. Write down all the experiences in your life that indicate there is a God. Think about all the ways God has directed you to your purposes (yes, more than one).

   - Do you believe God can do great things through your life?

Prayer

Dear God, help me trust you with all my heart. Increase my understanding of you and the plans you have for my life. Strengthen my ability to follow the path you set before me, even when it does not look clear. I believe you created me to do good on Earth. Today I embrace your quiet directions and subtle signs to pursue that which I do not fully comprehend. Amen.

Day 4: Believe

Spiritual Workout

1. Do you have people in your life that believe in you?
   - How have they encouraged and supported you to live your purpose?
   - Do you believe what they believe about you?
2. Make a list of all your personality traits that make you unique.
   - How does God want to use your unique traits?
   - How can you use your unique talents to bless someone's life today?

Prayer

Dear God, help me trust you with all my heart. Increase my understanding of you and the plans you have for my life. Strengthen my ability to follow the path you set before me even when it does not look clear. I believe you created me to do good on Earth. Today I embrace your quiet directions and subtle signs to pursue that which I do not fully comprehend. Amen.

Day 5: Believe

Spiritual Workout

1. If you died today, would you feel like you accomplished what God called you to do on Earth?
   - Why or why not?
   - How much time do you believe you have?
2. What do you believe people would say about you at your funeral?
   - What do you want people to say about you?
   - What legacy do you want to leave after you have passed from this physical realm?

Prayer

Dear God, help me trust you with all my heart. Increase my understanding of you and the plans you have for my life. Strengthen my ability to follow the path you set before me, even when it does not look clear. I believe you created me to do good on Earth. Today I embrace your quiet directions and subtle signs to pursue that which I do not fully comprehend. Amen.

Day 6: Believe

Spiritual Workout

1. What motivates you to get up every day?
2. What passions are you currently pursuing that keep you vibrant and excited about life?
3. Do you believe you are living life to the fullest?
   - If so, how? If not, why not?
4. Make a list of all the fun and outrageous things you want to do or experience.
   - Put a star next to the top three.
   - Schedule time to accomplish them over the next six months.

Prayer

Dear God, help me trust you with all my heart. Increase my understanding of you and the plans you have for my life. Strengthen my ability to follow the path you set before me, even when it does not look clear. I believe you created me to do good on Earth. Today I embrace your quiet directions and subtle signs to pursue that which I do not fully comprehend. Amen.

Day 7: Believe

Spiritual Workout

1. What are you believing God for right now? (Ex. A promotion at work, better health, etc.)
2. Are you believing that God will use you to make your home, community, or world better? If so, how?
3. Are you willing to believe God for something big? (If so, write it down)
4. What would be different about your life and the world around you if you truly believed in a power greater than yourself?

Prayer

Dear God, help me trust you with all my heart. Increase my understanding of you and the plans you have for my life. Strengthen my ability to follow the path you set before me even when it does not look clear. I believe you created me to do good on Earth. Today I embrace your quiet directions and subtle signs to pursue that which I do not fully comprehend. Amen.

PRINCIPLE TWO: SENSES

"Just as we must open our eyes—must raise our lids—to see, we must raise our barriers and open our hearts and minds if we are to see and feel the essence of the life around us."

–Mark Nepo

Have you ever had a conversation with someone when you could hear their words but actually felt they were communicating something different? Maybe you have been in a group and noticed a person's body language did not match what they were saying. You may have thought to yourself, "Huh, that was odd." Have *you* ever spoken with someone and your words were not in alignment with what you were feeling or wanted to communicate? Think about it. What was happening in those moments? What was that intangible exchange you experienced but could not quite explain?

Principle Two is about the intangible "thing" that happens when people communicate with one another. That "thing" is like the sound waves we cannot see but we can hear and like the heat waves, we feel but cannot touch. In simple terms, it is the essence of communication. It is a deeper message that can only be filtered through the power of your senses. Your ability to "see" and "listen" beyond what you observe with your eyes and hear with your ears. As the saying goes, "There is more to this than meets the eye." Your senses are critical to your spiritual development and how you navigate the world around you.

> "But blessed are your eyes, for they see;
> and your ears, for they hear."
> –Proverbs 13:16

Your senses, particularly your sight and hearing, are vital to your spiritual and social-emotional development. In most early childhood classrooms, you will see a picture of hands, eyes, ears, a nose, and a mouth on the wall. It is one of the first visual representations used to teach children about the five senses of touch, sight, hearing, smell, and taste. From that stage forward, you go through life believing your five senses are the only tools you use to assess your environment. However, no one ever says, "I learned my ABC's so I don't really need to learn how to utilize letters, comprehend words, apply vocabulary, and synthesize my thoughts in written form." That would be strange, right? The development of your senses is just as crucial to your existence as developing reading and writing skills. You use your senses to communicate with God, yourself, and others.

Take, for instance, the mentoring support my husband and I have provided to couples. Many couples have come to us with the belief that their relationship is faltering due to issues such as infidelity, finances, children, loss of intimacy, and other external factors. That is true to a degree. However, when we look deeper and closer at the presented issue(s) we find another factor that may be less obvious, but very significant. Can you guess what that factor would be? Communication!

Within a few minutes of meeting with a couple, my husband and I can see an underlying breakdown in communication beneath the strained relationship. We notice that in conversations and arguments, the couple is talking at each other instead of to each other. It is our job to slow the couple down and bring their awareness to what is really being said by their partner. We get them to *see* and *listen* at a deeper level in order to create a beautiful connection through communication.

> "...the motivations of those who consciously sacrifice their lives for higher purposes make sense, the power of Gandhi is explicable, and the compassionate acts of the Christ are comprehensible in a fullness that is not accessible to the five-sensory human."
>
> –Gary Zukav

You can spend your life learning how to respond to what you experience with your physical eyes and ears but never actually learn how to comprehend what is being communicated at a deeper level. So much that happens in an exchange between people is about the intangible and invisible messages at a deeper level, beyond the five senses.

> "Everything we do, every relationship we have, succeeds or fails based on our level of true spiritual connection."
>
> –Oprah Winfrey

Imagine you are standing in the grocery check-out line. You do not know why, but on this day, the store is extremely crowded. The cashier seems overwhelmed, so much so that she looks like she might just walk off her shift. As she finishes with the customer in front of you, you ask her, "Are you okay?" As she looks at you, her demeanor immediately shifts from one of anger and frustration to one of despair. She responds, "I am going to pee on myself. I asked to go to the bathroom twenty minutes ago and my manager told me to wait."

I was that customer. I immediately offered to call her manager and ask if she could go to the bathroom while I wait. She said, "Thank you, miss! You are so kind. Everyone has been so disrespectful to me today." At that moment, I sought to understand the emotion behind her emotions, the meaning behind her behaviors, and the feelings behind her words.

What would happen if you spoke less, asked more, and listened to understand instead of listening to respond? What would happen if you took the time to observe not just a person's behavior but the possible intentions behind their behaviors? You can see love, anger, frustration, compassion, empathy, trust, disappointment, fatigue, and excitement if you listen with more than your ears and see with more than your eyes.

To be *spiritually woke* is to live life with a greater awareness beyond the five senses you know. Your five senses are especially important but can limit your spiritual growth and hinder the impact you can have on people around you. Choose to see and listen at a deeper level!

Day 1: Senses

Spiritual Workout

1. Think back to a time when you sensed something that was not explicit or overt. (Ex. Maybe you felt or heard something while having a conversation with your manager at work.)

    - What do you believe was being communicated at that moment?

2. Spend the next couple of days "listening" to and "seeing" people. Practice talking less and asking more questions so you are not on "autopilot" in your interactions.

Prayer

Dear God, I ask that you heighten my ability to listen and see all that is happening around me. Awaken my spirit to the intangible messages being communicated to me every day. Help me take time to listen more and ask so I can have a deeper understanding of people and our interactions. Today I acknowledge that I am more than my five senses. Amen.

Day 2: Senses

Spiritual Workout

1. Have you ever made a life decision that was solely based on the intangible "thing" referenced in this chapter?
   - If so, what was the decision?
2. Try this activity with a friend. Choose a safe space free from large objects. With your eyes closed, have your friend stand in a spot in the room. Without using sight, slowly see if you can find your friend. This activity will highlight the importance of slowing down and becoming aware of the intangibles.

Prayer

Dear God, I ask that you heighten my ability to listen and see all that is happening around me. Awaken my spirit to the intangible messages being communicated to me every day. Help me take time to listen more and ask so I can have a deeper understanding of people and our interactions. Today I acknowledge that I am more than my five senses. Amen.

Day 3: Senses

Spiritual Workout

1. Listen to a piece of classical or meditation music. Sit quietly without distraction. Begin to pay attention to more than the notes.
   - Write down what you hear and see.
2. When you wake up tomorrow, before you get out of bed, pause. Take a moment to awaken all your senses before immediately jumping into the day's responsibilities. Look around your room and listen to the sounds around you and ask yourself the critical question, "What do I want from this day?"

Prayer

Dear God, I ask that you heighten my ability to listen and see all that is happening around me. Awaken my spirit to the intangible messages being communicated to me every day. Help me take time to listen more and ask so I can have a deeper understanding of people and our interactions. Today I acknowledge that I am more than my five senses. Amen.

Day 4: Senses

Spiritual Workout

1. If you had to quantify your time, as a percentage, on a given day:
   - How much time are you aware of what is happening around you?
   - How much time are you on "autopilot"?
2. Do you "see" people when you are in conversation with them?
3. Do you intentionally set aside time in your day to just be quiet?
4. Have you ever fasted from social media?
   - Select some time one day per week (blocks of time in the day) to disconnect from social media.

Prayer

Dear God, I ask that you heighten my ability to listen and see all that is happening around me. Awaken my spirit to the intangible messages being communicated to me every day. Help me take time to listen more and ask so I can have a deeper understanding of people and our interactions. Today I acknowledge that I am more than my five senses. Amen.

Day 5: Senses

Spiritual Workout

1. Make a list of the local or global issues that "speak" to you.
   - Why do these issues bother you?
2. In the *Day 1: Believe - Principle Workout* you were asked to make a list of leaders you admire.
   - Select one of the leaders, find a video or audio clip of them giving a speech, talk, or sermon.
   - Engage your senses by listening to them.
   - What are they communicating beyond their words and behaviors?
   - What do you feel when you listen to them?

Prayer

Dear God, I ask that you heighten my ability to listen and see all that is happening around me. Awaken my spirit to the intangible messages being communicated to me every day. Help me take time to listen more and ask so I can have a deeper understanding of people and our interactions. Today I acknowledge that I am more than my five senses. Amen.

Day 6: Senses

Spiritual Workout

1. Select someone in your life who annoys you. Choose the setting (in-person, video chat, text, etc.) and ask them the following questions:
   - Do you know why you were born?
   - What do you hope to accomplish before you leave this life?
   - If you could change one thing about yourself what would it be and why?
   - Be sure to listen, listen, listen! Pay attention! Focus for the intangible!

Prayer

Dear God, I ask that you heighten my ability to listen and see all that is happening around me. Awaken my spirit to the intangible messages being communicated to me every day. Help me take time to listen more and ask so I can have a deeper understanding of people and our interactions. Today I acknowledge that I am more than my five senses. Amen.

Day 7: Senses

Spiritual Workout

1. Today, tune out the noise of the world, and the distraction of your phone, and spend one hour in silence.
    - Use the quiet time to focus your attention on the purpose God has for your life.
2. Go for a walk alone and observe your surroundings.
    - What do you hear?
    - What do you see?
    - Reflect on God's creation, including you.

Prayer

Dear God, I ask that you heighten my ability to listen and see all that is happening around me. Awaken my spirit to the intangible messages being communicated to me every day. Help me take time to listen more and ask so I can have a deeper understanding of people and our interactions. Today I acknowledge that I am more than my five senses. Amen.

PRINCIPLE THREE: GRATITUDE

"Every good and perfect gift is from above, coming down from the Father of the heavenly lights, who does not change like shifting shadows."

–James 1:17

When was the last time you expressed gratitude for the air you breathe, the sun that shines, or the stars that twinkle at night? When you woke up this morning, did you stop and express gratitude for life? When you reflect on yesterday, do you stop and voice appreciation for the little things? From the moment you open your eyes until you rest your head at night, God blesses you with countless gifts. We could spend the entire day thanking Him for the basic functions of our body alone!

Principle three focuses on gratitude which is the state of being grateful. Being grateful is more than just saying *thank you* to someone for a gift or an act of kindness. Gratitude is a deeper emotion and a connection to your life experiences, people, places, and things. Being grateful or expressing gratitude comes from the recesses of your heart. It can be spoken without words, stated without gestures, and felt without touch. To be *spiritually woke* you *must* develop a daily practice of being grateful and expressing gratitude. As common as it sounds, gratitude is an attitude and way of life.

The academic fields of Positive Psychology and Religious Studies have invested a lot of resources into the study of gratitude. Some of the research has linked gratitude to benefits like increased physical and emotional health, better sleep, and an overall happier disposition. If you feel uninspired about your life, practicing gratitude would be a wise practice to implement. While it may seem simple, it is one of the most powerful forces in the universe. Embodying gratitude can turn enemies into friends and defeat into triumph. When you express appreciation for your life experiences, you tap into a power that transcends the physical realm.

> **"The miracle of gratitude is that it shifts your perception to such an extent that it changes the world you see."**
>
> –Dr. Robert Holden

Could you imagine that losing your job would be the best thing to ever happen to you? Is it possible that the loss of a long-term friendship could transform your life for good? How you choose to think about the job loss will determine the experience you have moving forward in your next career path. The lessons learned and joyful experiences of your friendship will help you navigate future relationships. Being grateful for all that occurs in your life helps you remember that nothing is happening *to* you but happening *for* you.

When you focus your attention on the challenges of life you can miss the miracles God has set up for you. That is not to say you cannot experience disappointments. You will have moments of great anger or frustration from situations that are unfair and overwhelming. The point is, disappointment should not consume you to the point that you miss the messages and gifts that can stem from turmoil. You do not need to look far to hear testimonies of people finding better jobs after a termination, falling in love after a horrible break-up, or starting over after hitting rock bottom. Being grateful shifts how you see tribulation and provides new insight into your life.

Sometimes you can get lost in the details of your life but living with a spirit of gratitude makes you aware of the bigger picture.

> "Cultivate the habit of being grateful for every good thing that comes to you and give thanks continuously. And because all things have contributed to your advancement, you should include all things in your gratitude."
>
> –Ralph Waldo Emerson

Being grateful is a habit. The more you integrate it into your human existence, the quicker it becomes a part of your character. Your habits rule your life. If you have a habit of being late, you will begin to live by that habit and then others will associate you with that habit. If you have a habit of being judgmental, you will constantly find things to judge.

The same goes for the habit of compassion. If you practice compassion with others and yourself, you will see and experience compassion. You can always find something to be grateful for if you choose to be grateful in all circumstances.

> "It is through gratitude for the present moment that the spiritual dimension of life opens up."
>
> –Eckhart Tolle

As mentioned earlier, losing my job was a major catalyst for my spiritual growth. Gratitude was one of the traits that emerged during this period of my life. I expressed gratitude for the job opportunity, for what I learned in the process, for who

I became through the process, *and* for the possibilities ahead of me. I thanked God for the people I met and the situations that challenged me. At the very moment I received the news of my termination, I chose gratitude. Do you hear me? I chose it! I released God's power in my life by choosing a spirit of gratitude. From that choice came this book and many other new experiences in my career.

My mother, an incredibly wise woman, always says, "There is no such thing as tomorrow, for when a so-called tomorrow comes, it is in fact today." Being *spiritually woke* helps you recognize that the present moment is the most powerful resource you have. You cannot change what has already occurred and what is to come is influenced by the present. So, wherever you find yourself at this moment, be grateful.

Pause.

Reflect.

Acknowledge how far you have come and show appreciation for the breath in your body. You are still alive and you have been granted another opportunity to be a blessing. Do not waste it murmuring and complaining about things you cannot control. Choose gratitude!

Day 1: Gratitude

Spiritual Workout

1. Make a list of at least five things you are grateful for that occurred during the day.
2. Reflect on a challenging situation that has happened in your life (past or present).
   - Write down what you have learned about yourself through the situation.
   - Write three reasons to be grateful for the situation.
3. Write a thank-you note to someone who touched your life today. It can also be a text or social media message.

Prayer

My God, today I thank you with all my heart, soul, mind, and strength for the blessings you have bestowed upon me and my loved ones. I express my deepest gratitude for my life. Today, help me to shift my focus to the goodness in my life and appreciate the lessons you have for me. I have breath in my body, so I praise you for my life. I am grateful for life! Amen.

Day 2: Gratitude

Spiritual Workout

1. Make a list of at least five things you are grateful for that occurred during the day.
2. Make a list of five family members.
3. Complete the following sentence for each one: "I am grateful for [family member's name], because…"
4. Write a thank-you note to someone who touched your life today. (It can also be a text or social media message.)

Prayer

My God, today I thank you with all my heart, soul, mind, and strength for the blessings you have bestowed upon me and my loved ones. I express my deepest gratitude for my life. Today, help me to shift my focus to the goodness in my life and appreciate the lessons you have for me. I have breath in my body, so I praise you for my life. I am grateful for life! Amen.

Day 3: Gratitude

Spiritual Workout

1. Make a list of at least five things you are grateful for that occurred during the day.
2. Go for a gratitude walk alone or with a friend.
   - Pay attention to what you see.
   - Express gratitude for the beautiful nature around you.
3. Write a thank-you note to someone who touched your life today. It can also be a text or social media message.

Prayer

My God, today I thank you with all my heart, soul, mind, and strength for the blessings you have bestowed upon me and my loved ones. I express my deepest gratitude for my life. Today, help me to shift my focus to the goodness in my life and appreciate the lessons you have for me. I have breath in my body, so I praise you for my life. I am grateful for life! Amen.

Day 4: Gratitude

Spiritual Workout

1. Make a list of at least five things you are grateful for that occurred during the day.
2. Start a gratitude chain.
   - Send a separate message to three friends sharing a reason you are grateful for their friendship.
   - Ask the friends you have chosen to send gratitude messages to three friends of their choosing.
2. Write a thank-you note to someone who touched your life today. It can also be a text or social media message.

Prayer

My God, today I thank you with all my heart, soul, mind, and strength for the blessings you have bestowed upon me and my loved ones. I express my deepest gratitude for my life. Today, help me to shift my focus to the goodness in my life and appreciate the lessons you have for me. I have breath in my body, so I praise you for my life. I am grateful for life! Amen.

Day 5: Gratitude

Spiritual Workout

1. Make a list of at least five things you are grateful for that occurred during the day.
2. Pay your gratitude forward. Find a stranger and do something kind for him or her like buy a cup of coffee, buy a bus token, pay for extra time on their parking meter, etc.
3. Write a thank-you note to someone who touched your life today. It can also be a text or social media message.

Prayer

My God, today I thank you with all my heart, soul, mind, and strength for the blessings you have bestowed upon me and my loved ones. I express my deepest gratitude for my life. Today, help me to shift my focus to the goodness in my life and appreciate the lessons you have for me. I have breath in my body, so I praise you for my life. I am grateful for life! Amen.

Day 6: Gratitude

Spiritual Workout

1. Make a list of at least five things you are grateful for that occurred during the day.
2. Close your eyes and take a few minutes to focus on your physical body, from your toes to your head.
   - Pay attention to your breathing.
   - Begin to thank God for sustaining your life.

Prayer

My God, today I thank you with all my heart, soul, mind, and strength for the blessings you have bestowed upon me and my loved ones. I express my deepest gratitude for my life. Today, help me to shift my focus to the goodness in my life and appreciate the lessons you have for me. I have breath in my body, so I praise you for my life. I am grateful for life! Amen.

Day 7: Gratitude

Spiritual Workout

1. Make a list of at least five things you are grateful for that occurred during the day.
2. Walk around your home and silently observe the "feel" of it and the objects within it.
   - Express gratitude for the things that make your house feel like a home (furniture, pictures, people, food, family game night, Thanksgiving, etc.)
3. Write a thank-you note to someone who touched your life today. It can also be a text or social media message.

Prayer

My God, today I thank you with all my heart, soul, mind, and strength for the blessings you have bestowed upon me and my loved ones. I express my deepest gratitude for my life. Today, help me to shift my focus to the goodness in my life and appreciate the lessons you have for me. I have breath in my body, so I praise you for my life. I am grateful for life! Amen.

PRINCIPLE FOUR: THOUGHTS

If you think you are beaten, you are.
If you think you dare not, you don't.
If you'd like to win, but you think you can't,
It is almost a cinch - you won't.

If you think you'll lose, you've lost.
For out in this world we find,
Success begins with a fellow's will,
It's all in the state of mind.

If you think you're outclassed, you are.
You've got to think high to rise.
You've got to be sure of yourself before
You can ever win the prize.

Life's battles don't always go
To the stronger or faster man.
But sooner or later the man who wins
Is the one who thinks he can!

—Walter Wintle

My role as a parent is to give my children tools that will support them in becoming who God designed them to be. I began teaching my little ones the aforementioned Walter Wintle poem from the moment they could speak. I wanted them to have it memorized by the time they went to kindergarten. Now, they say it every morning before heading off to school. It is one way I help to illustrate for them that their thinking affects their life.

Have you ever heard someone say, "I can see your thoughts?" It is an interesting statement, isn't it? Think about it. How can you see a person's thoughts? Is there a way to assess how healthy a person's thoughts are?

When I was younger, my mom would tell my brothers and me, "Watch your thoughts, they become things." As children, it was a difficult statement to comprehend. How exactly did she think we could watch our thoughts? Were we supposed to go in a corner and sit quietly while our thoughts drifted by in front of us like on a movie screen? As we got older, we gained a better understanding of the spiritual practice of "watching our thoughts." What our mom meant by "watch" was to observe and be attentive, to monitor our ideas and feelings. She taught us that our words and behaviors followed our thoughts.

> "No action is possible without thought, and no great action is possible until a great thought has preceded it."
>
> –Wallace D. Wattles

Being mindful of your thoughts is an integral part of living a *spiritually woke* life. Your thoughts are a blueprint for your world. *Everything, first, begins with a thought.* For example, before a contractor can begin a project on a house, he or she must first understand what the homeowner envisions for their space. Their thoughts must be transferred into something tangible for the contractor to use as a guide. Before ground is broken or a nail is hammered, those initial thoughts must become the blueprint for the project. The contractor takes the homeowner's thoughts and turns them into a drawing. The thoughts have now become a "thing."

Great movies, heart-warming music, grassroots movements, and New York Times' best-selling books all began as a thought. Before an author writes one word, they have thoughts or visions about the story. The same concept applies to things like war, assassinations of civil rights and political leaders, *and* slavery. Those too started with a thought in the mind of one person.

> "Finally, brothers and sisters, whatever is true, whatever is noble, whatever is right, whatever is pure, whatever is lovely, whatever is admirable—if anything is excellent or praiseworthy—think about such things."
>
> –Philippians 4:8

It is important to understand that a thought can create peace or it can bring destruction to a person, family, community, or country. Thoughts have POWER! *Your* thoughts have POWER! You are either creating harmony or chaos with your thought power.

What thoughts have been driving your daily life? Are your thoughts taking you closer to your dreams or deeper into despair? Are you allowing the negative thinking of others to influence you?

Take a moment to look at your life in its current state. Look at your relationships, finances, career, health and overall life satisfaction. How do you feel about what you see? Where is the blueprint for the life you are experiencing and when did you start creating that blueprint? (Tough right?)

> "Regardless of what it is you feel you should have more of, whether it be wealth, success, health, better relations with others, or more sales, they all resolve themselves back to a thought pattern."
>
> –Willis Kinnear

I have many examples of how I thought things into my life. One of my favorite stories occurred during my early twenties while I was completing my master's degree. One day on my way to class, I saw a silver Honda Civic coupe just off the lot. I am not sure why it caught my attention but I was so enamored by it, I decided it would be my next car. From that day forth, every time I saw a Honda Civic coupe, I saw myself driving a silver one with a sunroof and other top-of-the-line amenities. The thoughts became so vivid, I began seeing new, silver Civics every day. There was never a doubt in my mind that I would have that car.

Eventually, the day came when the lease on my current car ended and I needed to get a new one. While on the phone with the car dealership, a salesman asked if I knew what vehicle I wanted next. Without hesitation, I said, "I want a Honda Civic." There was a five-second pause before he said, "Wow, we just got a brand new, never been driven, Honda Civic." I think I must have leapt out of my body, ran around the room, and sat back down right before he said, "I hope you like silver." The car was delivered to my apartment with only six miles on the odometer. Everything I thought and envisioned was now in a material form in front of my eyes—sunroof and all.

Your current desire may not be a new car. Perhaps it is a new job or a fulfilling and romantic relationship. Maybe you want to run for political office, start a non-profit organization, or transform the American educational system. Whatever you are envisioning for yourself, manifestation first begins with your thoughts.

> "...as quickly as light illuminates a room, a single thought can shed new light on your life, changing everything including your destiny."
>
> –Dr. Cindy Trimm

I can or I can't! I should or I shouldn't! I will or I won't! As simple as these statements are, each one represents a single thought, one that can shape the trajectory of your life. Being *spiritually woke* is about more than believing in God. It is about recognizing your God-given power to think thoughts that will transform your perspective on life and the lives of those around you. You may not be able to change a situation but you can change how you *think* about the situation. You may not be able to change what other people think about you but you can change the thoughts you have towards yourself.

> "For as a man thinketh in his heart, so is he..."
>
> –Proverbs 23:7

Day 1: Thoughts

Spiritual Workout

1. Journal about the different parts of the blueprint you have for your life—health, family, relationships, career, finances, community, spirituality etc.
   - How do these areas of your life currently look?
   - How do you want them to look in the future?
2. Answer the following question in your journal or in a notebook: Do my current thoughts support or destroy my blueprint?

Prayer

Heavenly Father, today I focus on thoughts that build experiences of love and peace. I recognize that I am a co-creator with you and my thoughts have power. Grant me a greater awareness of those thoughts that block the manifestation of my desires. Today I choose to use my thought-power to transform my life and the lives of those around me. Amen.

Day 2: Thoughts

Spiritual Workout

1. Find some powerful quotes that promote and support the type of life experiences you want.
   - Put the quotes on easily-accessible index cards or use an app to take a picture of the quote and use it as your phone and computer screensaver.
2. Find a new book that can fuel your passion and teach you something new about an area in your blueprint and begin reading it.

Prayer

Heavenly Father, today I focus on thoughts that build experiences of love and peace. I recognize that I am a co-creator with you and my thoughts have power. Grant me a greater awareness of those thoughts that block the manifestation of my desires. Today I choose to use my thought-power to transform my life and the lives of those around me. Amen.

Day 3: Thoughts

Spiritual Workout

1. In the morning and at night, take five minutes to sit in silence.
2. Visualize aspects of your blueprint and create a mental picture of how you'd desire your life to look.
3. Ask four friends the following question: What are four adjectives you would use to describe me?
   - Write down their answers.
   - Do you see any themes? If so, write them down.

Prayer

Heavenly Father, today I focus on thoughts that build experiences of love and peace. I recognize that I am a co-creator with you and my thoughts have power. Grant me a greater awareness of those thoughts that block the manifestation of my desires. Today I choose to use my thought-power to transform my life and the lives of those around me. Amen.

Day 4: Thoughts

Spiritual Workout

1. In the morning and at night, take five minutes to sit in silence.
2. Visualize aspects of your blueprint and create a mental picture of how you'd desire your life to look.
3. Ask four different friends the following question: What are four adjectives you would use to describe me?
   - Write down their answers.
   - Do you see any similarities with descriptions from your other four friends?
   - Do their thoughts align with the thoughts you have about yourself?

Prayer

Heavenly Father, today I focus on thoughts that build experiences of love and peace. I recognize that I am a co-creator with you and my thoughts have power. Grant me a greater awareness of those thoughts that block the manifestation of my desires. Today I choose to use my thought-power to transform my life and the lives of those around me. Amen.

Day 5: Thoughts

Spiritual Workout

1. In the morning and at night, take five minutes to sit in silence.
   - Visualize aspects of your blueprint and create a mental picture of how you'd desire your life to look.
2. Declutter your mind, Part 1:
   - On small pieces of paper, write down the thoughts that hinder you from pursuing your dreams. (Ex. not good enough, too old, not smart enough, do not have the resources)
   - Put the papers in an envelope.

Prayer

Heavenly Father, today I focus on thoughts that build experiences of love and peace. I recognize that I am a co-creator with you and my thoughts have power. Grant me a greater awareness of those thoughts that block the manifestation of my desires. Today I choose to use my thought-power to transform my life and the lives of those around me. Amen.

Day 6: Thoughts

Spiritual Workout

1. In the morning and at night, take five minutes to sit in silence.
   - Visualize aspects of your blueprint and create a mental picture of how you'd desire your life to look.
2. Declutter your mind, Part 2:
   - Take the envelope from yesterday and remove the pieces of paper.
   - On the back of each piece, write a statement that counters the thought. (Ex. I am more than enough, age is just a number, I can ask for help, etc.)

Prayer

Heavenly Father, today I focus on thoughts that build experiences of love and peace. I recognize that I am a co-creator with you and my thoughts have power. Grant me a greater awareness of those thoughts that block the manifestation of my desires. Today I choose to use my thought-power to transform my life and the lives of those around me. Amen.

Day 7: Thoughts

Spiritual Workout

1. In the morning and at night, take five minutes to sit in silence.
   - Visualize aspects of your blueprint and create a mental picture of how you'd desire your life to look.
2. Declutter your mind, Part 3:
   - In your journal or on a piece of paper, write down the statements you wrote from yesterday.
   - Tear up the pieces of paper and throw it in the garbage.
   - In your visualization activity, focus on these empowering statements.

Prayer

Heavenly Father, today I focus on thoughts that build experiences of love and peace. I recognize that I am a co-creator with you and my thoughts have power. Grant me a greater awareness of those thoughts that block the manifestation of my desires. Today I choose to use my thought-power to transform my life and the lives of those around me. Amen.

PRINCIPLE FIVE: WORDS

*"The power of the tongue is life and death—
those who love to talk will eat what it produces."*

—*Proverbs 18:21*

Your thoughts are the blueprint for your life. So, if thoughts represent the plan for your life, your words are the materials used to bring that plan into fruition. Every time you speak you are communicating your vision for the world around you while simultaneously creating that world. Like thoughts, your words can be used to form a life filled with inspiration or one consumed with defeat because, through your words, you give meaning to your life. You have the power to speak peace or chaos, blessings or curses, abundance or lack. Your words follow your thoughts.

Words are transformative and have the ability to change a person's experience, a community, a nation, and the planet. One of the most iconic speeches in history, and the epitome of being *spiritually woke*, was the "I Have a Dream" speech delivered on August 28, 1963, by Dr. Martin Luther King Jr. In seventeen minutes, Dr. King shared a blueprint, not just for his family, for the global community. From that speech, he created hope, inspiration, compassion, and change. His words, as they had done numerous times before, triggered something that caused people to stop, pay attention, reflect, and act. Forty-five years later, the transformative power of that speech still exists. The words have been repeated millions of times over, by children and adults, around the world for the purpose of promoting transformation. Although he has passed on from this life, his presence continues to be felt through his speeches. When Dr. King had the option to speak life, he spoke!

> **"You are an outward expression of your deepest thoughts, emotions, and inward beliefs that you hold to be true about yourself. What you see about yourself is what you say about yourself."**
>
> **–Dr. Lucille Farrell-Scott**

It has been said that "I Am" is one of the most powerful statements one can speak. In the Bible's Old Testament, God instructed Moses to lead the children of Israel out of bondage. Moses asked God, "Behold, when I come unto the children of Israel, and shall say unto them, the God of your fathers hath sent me unto you; and they shall say to me, what is His name? What shall I say unto them?" God replied, "I AM THAT I AM" and He said, "Thus shalt thou say unto the children of Israel, *I AM* hath sent me unto you." In those five words, God articulated that He would be everything they needed.

I AM THAT I AM
(Replace 'THAT' with 'what' as needed)

In the New Testament, Jesus followed God's example by using "I Am" statements to describe who He was to be to the people.

"I Am the bread of life."

"I Am the good shepherd."

"I Am the light of the world."

These are just three of the seven "I Am" statements found in the New Testament of the Bible. What words do you put after your "I Am" statement? How do you describe yourself to the world? When you speak your "I am," those words travel and are heard by people who believe what you say, including you. You are the first person to hear your "I am." Are you intentional about the words that follow your "I am?" Does it accurately reflect who and what you want to be?

> **"Words are singularly the most powerful force available to humanity. We can choose to use this force constructively with words of encouragement or destructively using words of despair. Words have energy and power with the ability to help, to heal, to hinder, to hurt, to harm, to humiliate and to humble."**
>
> **–Yehuda Berg**

Words are an essential part of our society. We use them to communicate thoughts, ideas, beliefs, and emotions. Without them, we would be left with the task of developing another form of communication. Through words, laws are created and contracts are enforced. Societies were built on the ideas of men who decided to combine their collective thoughts and memorialize them on paper. With the stroke of a pen, what was once an idea becomes law. Systemic racism and other forms of human oppression were all propagated and normalized through the use of words. That is powerful! Entire groups of people have been killed through the beliefs of people who used their words to promote hate. Never underestimate the power of your words.

From the time you wake up in the morning until you lay your head down at night, you are engaging with words in written or spoken form. It is safe to say that between the media and your daily interactions with people, you are bombarded with all types of words. Being aware or *spiritually woke* to the messages you consciously and unconsciously receive is vital because the words can influence your behaviors and habits.

Think about the times you have heard gossip about someone and repeated it in a conversation with different people. Whether the information was true or not isn't the point. Words are like feathers in a bag, once you release them, the wind carries them far and wide and you can never get them back. With one click of a mouse or the press of a button, your words can create hope or invoke fear. In an instant, you no longer have control over the impact of your words because people are then able to make their own interpretations.

Do you know how many words you use per day? How would your life feel if there was a limit on the number of words you could use each day? Can you imagine being limited to speak the same number of characters allotted in an Instagram post? How intentional would you be?

> "Be impeccable with your word. Speak with integrity. Say only what you mean. Avoid using the word to speak against yourself or to gossip about others. Use the power of your word in the direction of truth and love."
>
> –Don Miguel Ruiz

What you speak, you and all those around you will believe. You are authoring your life every day in the same manner a writer pens a novel or a lyricist writes a verse. It is with the potential to invoke deep feelings and emotions from people. Your words have creative ability, so be intentional and thoughtful in how you use them.

Day 1: Words

Spiritual Workout

1. Be mindful of the words you are speaking. Imagine that everything you said today would manifest itself instantly.
2. Reflect on your relationships in your journal or notebook and answer the following questions:
   - What type of words have I spoken about my personal and professional relationships?
   - Do my relationships reflect love and harmony?

Prayer

My God, help me to be aware of what I am creating with my words. Place a guard over my tongue to ensure I do not hurt myself or those around me. I know that I can decree a thing and it will be established so I choose words of peace and abundance. Today I remember that I have creative power in my DNA and I can inspire all those with whom I come in contact. Today I speak words of life. Amen.

Day 2: Words

Spiritual Workout

1. Take time to think about your core values – the things that matter to you (Ex. integrity, love, family, trust, friendship etc.).
   - Select five words that represent your core values.
   - Do your words align with how you speak every day?
2. Reflect on your health in your journal or notebook and answer the following questions:
   - What words have I used to describe my health and my body?
   - Do my words reflect life?

Prayer

My God, help me to be aware of what I am creating with my words. Place a guard over my tongue to ensure I do not hurt myself or those around me. I know that I can decree a thing and it will be established so I choose words of peace and abundance. Today I remember that I have creative power in my DNA and I can inspire all those with whom I come in contact. Today I speak words of life. Amen.

Day 3: Words

Spiritual Workout

1. Take an audit of the time you spend during the day listening to or reading words from other people (Ex. radio, television, social media, talking to friends, etc.).
   - Write down an estimate of the number and the quality of those words.
2. Reflect on your finances in your journal or notebook and answer the following questions:
   - What type of words do I use to describe my finances?
   - Do my words reflect what I want for my finances?

Prayer

My God, help me to be aware of what I am creating with my words. Place a guard over my tongue to ensure I do not hurt myself or those around me. I know that I can decree a thing and it will be established so I choose words of peace and abundance. Today I remember that I have creative power in my DNA and I can inspire all those with whom I come in contact. Today I speak words of life. Amen.

Day 4: Words

Spiritual Workout

1. Choose at least two people you want to inspire today through your words. Feel free to select strangers or friends.

   - Be intentional about the words you use and communicate an inspirational message to them (via text, call, or face to face).

2. Reflect on your career in your journal or notebook and answer the following questions:

   - What type of words do I use to describe my career?
   - Do the words reflect what I want for my career?

Prayer

My God, help me to be aware of what I am creating with my words. Place a guard over my tongue to ensure I do not hurt myself or those around me. I know that I can decree a thing and it will be established so I choose words of peace and abundance. Today I remember that I have creative power in my DNA and I can inspire all those with whom I come in contact. Today I speak words of life. Amen.

Day 5: Words

Spiritual Workout

1. Spend at least thirty minutes in silence—no music, cell phone, television, or contact with anyone.
   - During your quiet time, reflect on the words you use to describe yourself.
2. Reflect on the words you use to describe yourself in your journal or notebook and answer the following questions:
   - What type of words do I use to describe myself?
   - Do the words reflect who I want to be?

Prayer

My God, help me to be aware of what I am creating with my words. Place a guard over my tongue to ensure I do not hurt myself or those around me. I know that I can decree a thing and it will be established so I choose words of peace and abundance. Today I remember that I have creative power in my DNA and I can inspire all those with whom I come in contact. Today I speak words of life. Amen.

Day 6: Words

Spiritual Workout

1. Pretend you are Dr. Martin Luther King, Jr. Using only seven sentences, write your version of the "I Have a Dream" speech for the current state of our society.
2. Reflect on your contribution to society in your journal or notebook and answer the following questions:
   - How can I be an inspiration to my community?
   - How can I make my "I Have a Dream" speech a reality?

Prayer

My God, help me to be aware of what I am creating with my words. Place a guard over my tongue to ensure I do not hurt myself or those around me. I know that I can decree a thing and it will be established so I choose words of peace and abundance. Today I remember that I have creative power in my DNA and I can inspire all those with whom I come in contact. Today I speak words of life. Amen.

Day 7: Words

Spiritual Workout

1. Write a powerful "I Am" statement for yourself that reflects your talents and the legacy you want to leave on Earth after you are gone. *Example: I am a creative and intuitive woman. I inspire people wherever I go and help people feel confident about themselves. I am blessed to be a blessing and God uses me to spread goodness and love.*
2. Make your "I Am" statement your daily mantra.

Prayer

My God, help me to be aware of what I am creating with my words. Place a guard over my tongue to ensure I do not hurt myself or those around me. I know that I can decree a thing and it will be established so I choose words of peace and abundance. Today I remember that I have creative power in my DNA and I can inspire all those with whom I come in contact. Today I speak words of life. Amen.

PRINCIPLE SIX: TRANSFORMATION

"Just when the caterpillar thought the world was over, she became a butterfly."

—Ancient Proverb

The word transformation is used frequently in conversations to reference personal growth, trials and tribulations, enlightenment, and spirituality. Go anywhere in the world and you will probably find people with tattoos of caterpillars and butterflies representing significant changes they may have experienced in life. It can be a beautiful image and testimony of the power and resilience of the human spirit.

However, it is interesting that when transformation or metamorphosis is referenced, there is usually a focus on a clear starting point (caterpillar) and final manifestation of change (butterfly). On a daily basis, we can find social media posts with quotes like, "What the caterpillar calls the end, the rest of the world calls a butterfly" by Lao Tsu. That's because most human beings like the idea of a miraculous transformation that appears to occur with ease, the operative word being "ease." As beautiful as it appears, the idea that you go from one phase to another without chaos or disruption is unrealistic. Nothing in nature changes without turmoil and detachment.

For obvious reasons, we highlight the two extremes. Everyone wants to hear about the humble beginning and powerful ending because it is sexy. Rarely do we give attention to the phase that happens right before the stunning butterfly emerges because that's not as sexy. Principle six is about valuing the phases of life that fall between the caterpillar and the butterfly, known as the chrysalis phase. To be *spiritually woke* is to know that life is not a series of starting and ending points but a journey of in-between. The extreme ends of your life experiences only tell part of your story. What happens along the way, in the middle, are the defining moments of your life's voyage.

> **"The butterfly emerges not from the perfectly formed caterpillar, but from the formless, vulnerable chrysalis."**
>
> –Dr. Sunne-Ryse Smith

For the caterpillar to transform into a butterfly it must undergo an in-between phase. This phase is so intense and is described as gruesome and radical. It is a strong period that forces the caterpillar to evolve, relinquish control, surrender to what it was and become something new. In the chrysalis phase, the caterpillar literally digests itself and dissolves its original form. It must destroy or let go of everything it thought it was so it can make room for something completely different. The chrysalis period is a transitional stage—a phase of uncertainty, chaos, frustration, disappointment, and discomfort—all prerequisites to transformation.

You, like the caterpillar, experience the discomfort of a chrysalis. The phase forces you to let go of who you thought you were so you can become the person you need to be in the next chapter of your life, a butterfly. When was the last time you experienced a chrysalis phase of life? Have you ever felt uncertain, confused, lost, or saddened in your professional or personal life? Who did you become on the journey? What did you learn about yourself? What old habits or people did you release to ensure transformation for your life?

"When we are young, we develop survival mechanisms that last too long and eventually become impediments to our growth."

–Jane Fonda

I have had many chrysalis phases over my blessed life. One transition period that challenged me to my core occurred when I released layers of myself that I thought defined me. Imagine taking your 1.5-carat engagement ring to a small jewelry shop in the Chinatown diamond district in New York City to sell for a fraction of its worth. Yep, that was me! At the time, my consulting work was not enough to maintain the lifestyle my husband and I had built and he assumed responsibility for keeping our family financially stable. I could see the look on my husband's face when I left the house to go into the city. I knew what that ring meant to him and the sacrifices he had made to buy it. During that time, he ate peanut butter and jelly sandwiches for a year and almost lost the apartment he shared with his best friend. Up until now, it was our secret.

I thought my ring defined me, much like my doctorate degree and professional experiences. I wore it like a badge of honor. Don't get me wrong, it was an exquisite ring. However, I was letting it wear me instead of me wearing it. It was at that moment that who I thought I was, became irrelevant. God stripped my caterpillar life away by forcing me to decide between the needs of my family or the fire and brilliance of a ring that was engraved with the words "A Love Supreme." In that shop in Chinatown, the jeweler questioned me several times by asking, "Are you sure you want to do this?" With tears in my eyes, I released who I thought I needed to be. It was more than just letting go of the ring. That experience caused me to see myself as more than just the things I acquired.

> **"In the process of letting go you will lose many things from the past, but you will find yourself."**
>
> –Deepak Chopra

As time passed during this chrysalis period of my life, I walked away from leadership roles that had helped me to mature spiritually but limited my ability to reach a broader group of people. I embraced my unique gift of inspiring people while letting go of the need to fit in a traditional career. It was one of the most uncomfortable, frustrating, emotionally-taxing periods of my life. I was humbled and egotistical, lost and inspired, all at the same time. The chrysalis phase was everything that I now understand it to be, an unformed "blob." It was a period of uncertainty filled with a range of emotions. Unfortunately, I couldn't rush through the experience. I had to allow the process to occur. I had to let go of who I was so I could become who God needed me to be.

> "We can't become what we need to be
> by remaining what we are."
>
> –Oprah Winfrey

The beauty of this phase is that you will cycle through it multiple times in your life. The more you embrace its ambiguity, the more powerful you become spiritually. Your greatest breakthroughs will occur when you are forced to journey through the chaos of your own existence and when you are challenged by people and things that no longer feel comfortable. The periods that will matter the most in your life will not be when everything feels effortless, but when you experience personal, radical transformation. It is when you are let go from your job and realize that you want a new career or a long-term relationship has ended and your life has been turned upside down. *Those* moments will motivate you to grow your faith, seek God in a deeper way, and be aware of your ever-evolving purpose in life.

Remember, do not try to avoid the chrysalis phase and do not try to speed it up. It is crucial for you to fulfill your God-given destiny.

Day 1: Transformation

Spiritual Workout

1. Make a list of some very challenging periods in your life.
   - Take ten minutes of quiet time to ask God what lessons you were supposed to learn from those periods.
2. In Spiritual Workout Four you were asked, "What is the biggest vision you have for yourself and the people around you?"
   - Are you on track for that vision to happen?
   - Why or why not?

Prayer

Gracious and loving God, I boldly come to you with gratitude and humility. I acknowledge you as the author and finisher of my life. You do all things well. Help me to remember that the plan you have for my life will require me to embrace the chaos of transformation. Just as you protect the vulnerable chrysalis, you watch over me with love and care. Amen.

Day 2: Transformation

Spiritual Workout

1. Take five minutes to look at old pictures of yourself (from five years or older).
   - What do you notice about yourself?
   - How have you changed physically, emotionally, mentally, and spiritually?
   - Write down what you notice.
2. Ask at least two friends or family members how you have changed over the last 5-10 years.
   - Ask them to describe what they believe you have learned from your life experiences.
   - Ask them to share their hope for you.

Prayer

Gracious and loving God, I boldly come to you with gratitude and humility. I acknowledge you as the author and finisher of my life. You do all things well. Help me to remember that the plan you have for my life will require me to embrace the chaos of transformation. Just as you protect the vulnerable chrysalis, you watch over me with love and care. Amen.

Day 3: Transformation

Spiritual Workout

1. Journal three things you want to change in your life but have avoided due to fear.
   - Why are you not making the change(s)?
   - What would be different if you made the change(s)?
2. This week, change one thing in your daily routine. (Ex. Get up earlier or go to bed earlier, wake up to inspiring music, take a different route to work, change your hairstyle.) DO SOMETHING DIFFERENT so you can experience something different!

Prayer

Gracious and loving God, I boldly come to you with gratitude and humility. I acknowledge you as the author and finisher of my life. You do all things well. Help me to remember that the plan you have for my life will require me to embrace the chaos of transformation. Just as you protect the vulnerable chrysalis, you watch over me with love and care. Amen.

Day 4: Transformation

Spiritual Workout

1. Look up the word "transformation" in a dictionary.
   - Write down what the word means for you.
   - How can you embrace transformation in your life?
2. Sit in a chair with your feet flat on the floor. Cross your arms as if you are waiting for something or someone. Sit this way for twenty seconds and then immediately cross your arms the other way.
   - How did it feel to switch your arms from the comfortable position to the new position?
   - Write down your thoughts.

Prayer

Gracious and loving God, I boldly come to you with gratitude and humility. I acknowledge you as the author and finisher of my life. You do all things well. Help me to remember that the plan you have for my life will require me to embrace the chaos of transformation. Just as you protect the vulnerable chrysalis, you watch over me with love and care. Amen.

Day 5: Transformation

Spiritual Workout

1. Write yourself a letter from the future by answering the following questions:
   - Who would you like to be in five years?
   - What would you say to your "now" self?
   - What would you tell yourself about the changes you have made and how those changes have transformed your life?
2. Read your "I Am" statement from your "Day 7: Words" Spiritual Workout.

Prayer

Gracious and loving God, I boldly come to you with gratitude and humility. I acknowledge you as the author and finisher of my life. You do all things well. Help me to remember that the plan you have for my life will require me to embrace the chaos of transformation. Just as you protect the vulnerable chrysalis, you watch over me with love and care. Amen.

Day 6: Transformation

Spiritual Workout

1. Make a list of all the things that *could* go right if you were to make changes that would create more joy and passion in your life.
2. Make another change to your daily routine.
   - Choose something that may make you uncomfortable but will have great benefit. (Ex. go to the gym, try a new workout routine, fast from sugar or junk food.)
   - Implement the change for 48 hours.

Prayer

Gracious and loving God, I boldly come to you with gratitude and humility. I acknowledge you as the author and finisher of my life. You do all things well. Help me to remember that the plan you have for my life will require me to embrace the chaos of transformation. Just as you protect the vulnerable chrysalis, you watch over me with love and care. Amen.

Day 7: Transformation

Spiritual Workout

1. Find a YouTube video on the life cycle of a monarch butterfly that includes the chrysalis.
   - Watch the video and write down what you see.
   - How does that transformation process mirror changes you have undergone in your life?
2. Answer this question: What action step can I take today that will begin to transform my life that my "future self" will hug me for?
   - Then take that step.

Prayer

Gracious and loving God, I boldly come to you with gratitude and humility. I acknowledge you as the author and finisher of my life. You do all things well. Help me to remember that the plan you have for my life will require me to embrace the chaos of transformation. Just as you protect the vulnerable chrysalis, you watch over me with love and care. Amen.

PRINCIPLE SEVEN: CONTRIBUTION

"The first question which the priest and the Levite asked was, 'If I stop to help this man, what will happen to me?' But... the good Samaritan reversed the question. 'If I do not stop to help this man, what will happen to him?'"

–Dr. Martin Luther King, Jr.

The quote is taken from Dr. King's "I've Been to the Mountaintop" speech, delivered the night before he was assassinated. In the prophetic speech, he references a well-known Bible story about the "Good Samaritan" (Luke 10:30-37) who helped a man who lay beaten in the street after he had been robbed. In the original Bible text, it is clear that the Samaritan was not the first person to come across the man in need of assistance. Two religious men, a priest and a Levite, walked past him earlier. In his speech, Dr. King eloquently asserts his own interpretation of what the priest, the Levite, and the Samaritan may have been thinking when they found the traveler trampled on the side of the road. Dr. King surmised that the priest and the Levite were concerned about their own well-being while the Samaritan focused on the well-being of the man. What would our society look like if we all stopped to check in on the well-being of those who have been "beaten" by life's circumstances?

> **"The best way to find yourself is to lose yourself in the service of others."**
> **–Mahatma Gandhi**

Being spiritually awakened or *spiritually woke* provides for a greater purpose than simply your personal gain. You can spend time reading books about faith and God, including The Bible, but if they do not help to reveal how your life should be used to help others, you have missed something. Having breath in your body is the only evidence you need to prove that God wants to use you for a greater good.

To be God's servant and a contributor to the world is to find yourself outside of yourself. If you, like me, spend a great deal of time on self-analysis and spiritual development then you know you can become too much of an academic and forget the importance of practical application. Serving others, making a contribution, and acting on what you believe, is the tangible manifestation of your inner spiritual work. In those moments, you begin to learn who you are as you become the Good Samaritan.

Your life is a blessing and a contribution to other people. That does not mean you need to become an activist or quit your job to go out and save the world by teaching in a different country (unless that is what your spirit is directing you to do). It does mean you have something amazing to offer in the way of service. That could simply be:

- speaking words of encouragement to colleagues in your office,
- teaching coding to bright young minds in communities where opportunity and access are limited, or
- feeding the many souls who need nourishment because they have fallen on difficult times.

You can start within your circle of influence. You won't need to look far to find people to serve and bless. Think about the family and friends you may eat Thanksgiving dinner with or those who you walk past on your way to work.

> "Aliveness happens in action."
> –Brendon Burchard

God created you to be a contribution to the planet. The very system that maintains your existence is built on it through reciprocity. Stop for a moment. Put your hand in front of your face, a couple of inches in front of your nose and mouth. What do you feel? When you exhale, where is the breath going? Can you "feel" your life?

You are alive *because* of contribution. The scientific process you learned about in elementary school, photosynthesis, illustrates it best. Through the process of photosynthesis, marine and land-based plant life take in the carbon dioxide produced by breathing organisms (like you) and release oxygen back into the atmosphere. Every time you take a breath you are taking from the system and contributing back to it. There is an exchange that results in a mutual benefit for all organisms. This exchange of gases is clearly a more complicated process than what was just explained, however, the point is simple. Your physical body is alive because each organism, including you, is doing their part. This is known as reciprocity.

In essence, the concept of "being a contribution" is occurring all around you in various forms, scientifically, spiritually, emotionally, and physically. Some contributions you can see, like donations to a charity or participation in a clothing drive. There are also contributions you cannot see with your natural eye, like photosynthesis or prayer. You may go through life believing you have nothing to offer but that cannot be more disconnected from the truth. Even when standing still, you are contributing to the planet because you are breathing. The very actions of inhaling and exhaling add to the world by sustaining life.

> **"What good is it, my brothers, if someone says he has faith but does not have works? Can that faith save him? If a brother or sister is poorly clothed and lacking in daily food, and one of you says to them, "Go in peace, be warmed and filled," without giving them the things needed for the body, what good is that? So also, faith by itself, if it does not have works, is dead."**
>
> **–James 2:14-17**

The world needs many things. All you have to do is go on social media or watch a news program and you will see people, communities, organizations, and industries thirsting for inspiration. What the world needs most is *spiritually woke* people willing to believe in God as more than a figurehead of a religion. God is bigger than any single religion. Your belief in God is not expressed through the words you speak. Your God is seen through the actions you take in His name. Don't *tell* people about your God, *show* them your God. How you contribute to society is an expression of the very God you claim to serve because saying you have faith means nothing without an outward illustration of your inward belief.

Your contribution to the world and your immediate circle (family, work, friends, neighborhood) is a gift that is only valuable when given. As you complete the last week of this journey, make it a point to BE a contribution. Be a full expression of the goodness of God. Take time to help the person that everyone else walks by or chose not to see. Seek to help those who have been marginalized by oppressive systems.

At the root of contribution is love. If we say we love God but do not express love to our fellow man or woman, do we really love God? Take all you have learned to become fully awake and go live *spiritually woke*.

Day 1: Contribution

Spiritual Workout

1. Look up the words "contribution" and "contribute" in a dictionary.
   - Write down all the ways you have contributed to the lives of others and give yourself permission to brag.
2. Call two close friends.
   - Share about this journey you have been on to live *spiritually woke*.
   - Ask them if there is anything they need from you.
   - Be a contribution to them by offering your assistance.

Prayer

God of all things, I come boldly and confidently to You. I recognize that I am a contribution. I know that my life is not my own and You desire for me to use my gifts and talents to be a blessing. Awaken my spirit today so that I can see and hear when and where I am needed. I know that every resource I need to serve others is already inside of me. My willingness to help others releases those resources. Amen.

Day 2: Contribution

Spiritual Workout

1. Make a list of your unique gifts and talents.
2. Write down an answer to the following questions:
   - How can my unique gifts and talents be used to help others?
   - Have I fully used my gifts to be a contribution?
3. Select one talent or gift from the list above and use it to help someone today. (Do not overthink it)

Prayer

God of all things, I come boldly and confidently to You. I recognize that I am a contribution. I know that my life is not my own and You desire for me to use my gifts and talents to be a blessing. Awaken my spirit today so that I can see and hear when and where I am needed. I know that every resource I need to serve others is already inside of me. My willingness to help others releases those resources. Amen.

Day 3: Contribution

Spiritual Workout

1. Make a list of at least ten people (fictitious, non-fictitious, living, dead, family, friend or celebrity) who have made positive contributions to our society.
   - Imagine what your world would be if they did not exist.
2. Today, be a contribution to a complete stranger. Do something meaningful and thoughtful for them.

Prayer

God of all things, I come boldly and confidently to You. I recognize that I am a contribution. I know that my life is not my own and You desire for me to use my gifts and talents to be a blessing. Awaken my spirit today so that I can see and hear when and where I am needed. I know that every resource I need to serve others is already inside of me. My willingness to help others releases those resources. Amen.

Day 4: Contribution

Spiritual Workout

1. Write down your answer to the following questions:
   - What problem(s) in the world makes me sad or angry?
   - What can I do about this problem but have not done yet? (The goal is not to be the answer to the problem but rather understand how you can contribute to making things better.)
2. Research organizations or people who may be involved in creating solutions for the problem you mentioned.
   - How can you help them?

Prayer

God of all things, I come boldly and confidently to You. I recognize that I am a contribution. I know that my life is not my own and You desire for me to use my gifts and talents to be a blessing. Awaken my spirit today so that I can see and hear when and where I am needed. I know that every resource I need to serve others is already inside of me. My willingness to help others releases those resources. Amen.

Day 5: Contribution

Spiritual Workout

1. Find out if any of your friends are involved in charitable work. Ask them how you can assist in spreading the word, raising money, or provide other support.
2. Today, be a contribution to a complete stranger. Do something meaningful and thoughtful for them.

Prayer

God of all things, I come boldly and confidently to You. I recognize that I am a contribution. I know that my life is not my own and You desire for me to use my gifts and talents to be a blessing. Awaken my spirit today so that I can see and hear when and where I am needed. I know that every resource I need to serve others is already inside of me. My willingness to help others releases those resources. Amen.

Day 6: Contribution

Spiritual Workout

1. What effect could your life have on others if you chose to live as a contribution?
2. How can the world be different because you are alive?
3. Create a "Contribution Challenge" on social media.
   - Ask your friends and family to do something meaningful and thoughtful for a stranger.
   - Tag at least ten people in the post and ask them to share it.
   - Use the hashtags #ContributionChallenge and #LiveSpirituallyWoke on social media.

Prayer

God of all things, I come boldly and confidently to You. I recognize that I am a contribution. I know that my life is not my own and You desire for me to use my gifts and talents to be a blessing. Awaken my spirit today so that I can see and hear when and where I am needed. I know that every resource I need to serve others is already inside of me. My willingness to help others releases those resources. Amen.

Day 7: Contribution

Spiritual Workout

1. Create a personal mission statement for your life that reflects the contribution you want to make and how you want to live each day.
   - *Example: I inspire people to live their God-given dreams and to use their gifts with confidence and purpose.*
   - Make it your daily affirmation along with your "I Am" statements.

Prayer

God of all things, I come boldly and confidently to You. I recognize that I am a contribution. I know that my life is not my own and You desire for me to use my gifts and talents to be a blessing. Awaken my spirit today so that I can see and hear when and where I am needed. I know that every resource I need to serve others is already inside of me. My willingness to help others releases those resources. Amen.

SPIRITUALLY WOKE PRINCIPLES

Believe in God

Use your senses to see and hear

Express gratitude

Watch your thoughts for they become things your words create

Embrace change

Be a contribution

FINAL THOUGHT

I AM AWAKE

(Excerpt from "I AM That: Prayers and Affirmations for Successful Living" by Dr. Lucille Farrell-Scott and Dr. Sunne-Ryse S. Smith)

I Am awake! I Am alive!
I Am living! I Am life! I Am full of life!
This is the day God has made just for me and I Am rejoicing in this day!
God started this day with me on his mind and I woke up excited to welcome this new day.
I Am alive and awake to walk out the promise of this beautiful day!
Today I Am a tree planted by streams of water.
Like the tree brings forth fruit, I experience success in all my endeavors.
Everything that will occur today helps me to blossom.
I Am a flower coming into bud!
I have been given another opportunity to live my best life and I will.
I stretch my hands wide and I proclaim for everyone to hear...
I Am full of life!
I Am life!
I Am living!
I Am awake!
I Am alive!
I Am that! That is who I Am!

About the Author
Sunne-Ryse Smith, Psy.D.

Named Sunne-Ryse because her mother believed she would be the "dawning of a new day" to everyone she met, Dr. Sunne-Ryse S. Smith is a transformational trainer, ordained minister, Doctor of Psychology, inspirational speaker and professional mentor and through her books, workshops, and mentoring programs, you will find a new day with plenty of inspiration, revelation, and spiritual insight.

A former Executive Director of a large urban school district and an accomplished, international professional development trainer, she empowers people to take bold risks and dream big. She combines her unique professional experiences with her passion for spiritual development to create breakthrough experiences.

She was featured in Essence magazine along with her mother for their powerful affirmation book, "I Am That – Prayers and Affirmations for Successful Living."

What's Next?

Are you looking for more inspiration? Being spiritually woke is not a destination, it is a journey. Just as breathing is a necessary, daily practice, so is spiritual development. Visit my website www.drsunneryse.com for information on upcoming live events, retreats and workshop dates. Join others as they learn, laugh, and grow together spiritually and emotionally.

Are you interested in achieving some God-sized dreams? Are you ready to awaken to a more fulfilling life? Enroll in my six-month mentoring program and watch your world transform as you increase your awareness of God and the purpose He has for your life.

www.ingramcontent.com/pod-product-compliance
Lightning Source LLC
Chambersburg PA
CBHW020143130526
44591CB00030B/179